W9-BOA-904

The Library of
NATIVE AMERICANS™

The Miwok
of California

Jack S. Williams

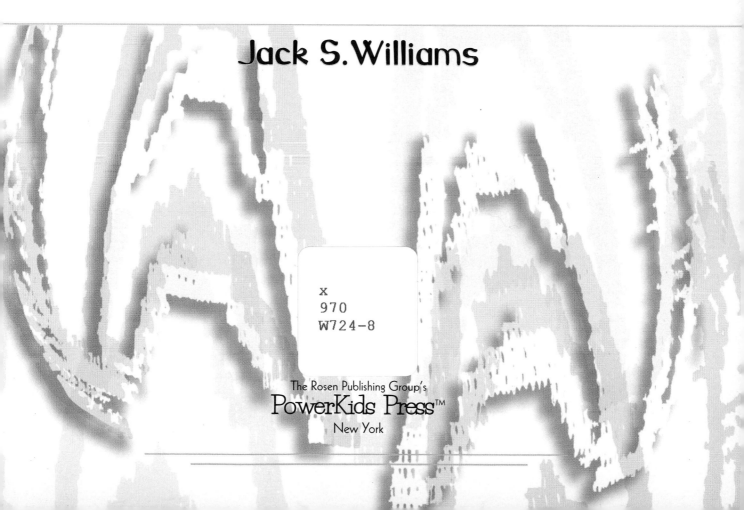

The Rosen Publishing Group's
PowerKids Press™
New York

For Mike Hardwick, who has always been a valued friend and a fellow voyager
on the journey to understanding the native peoples of early California

Published in 2004 by The Rosen Publishing Group, Inc.
29 East 21st Street, New York, NY 10010

Photo and illustration credits: cover, pp. 23, 26 courtesy of the Phoebe Apperson Hearst Museum of Anthropology and the Regents of the University of California; p. 6 © Jacques Langevin/Corbis Sygma; p. 8 © Royalty Free/Corbis; p. 10 courtesy of the Bancroft Library, University of California, Berkeley; pp. 13, 30, 50 National Anthropological Archives, Smithsonian Institution, Cat. No. 01528800, 03256400, 03259000, 09855000; pp. 16, 18, 19, 21, 24, 28, 34 courtesy of the C. Hart Merriam Collection of Native American Photographs, the Bancroft Library, University of California, Berkeley; p. 17 courtesy of Yosemite Museum, NPS; pp. 22, 52, 54, 56 © AP/Wide World Photos; p. 32 Northwestern University Library, Edward S. Curtis's *The Kato. The Wailaki. The Yuki. The Pomo. The Wintun. The Maidu. The Miwok. The Yokuts* [portfolio]; plate no. 496; pp. 36, 37, 38, 45, 46 © Hulton Archive/Getty Images; p. 41 courtesy of the Seaver Center for Western History Research, Natural History Museum of Los Angeles; pp. 43, 49 Library of Congress, Prints and Photographs Division; p. 47 courtesy of the California Heritage Collection, the Bancroft Library, University of California, Berkeley.

Designer: Geri Fletcher; Editor: Charles Hofer; Photo Researcher: Sherri Liberman

Williams, Jack S.
The Miwok of California / Jack S. Williams.
    p. cm. — (The library of Native Americans)
Includes bibliographical references and index.
Contents: Introducing the Miwok people — Daily life — Other aspects of Miwok life — Dealing with newcomers — The Miwok today.
ISBN 1-4042-2659-1 (lib. bdg.)
1. Miwok Indians—History—Juvenile literature. 2. Miwok Indians—Social life and customs—Juvenile literature. [1. Miwok Indians. 2. Indians of North America—California.] I. Title. II. Series.
E99.M69W55 2004
979.4004'974133—dc22

                                                                                    2003016622

Manufactured in the United States of America

A variety of terminologies has been employed in works about Native Americans. There are sometimes differences between the original names or terms used by a Native American group and the anglicized or modernized versions of such names or terms. Although this book contains terms that we feel will be most recognizable to our readership, there may also exist synonymous or native words that are preferred by certain speakers.

Contents

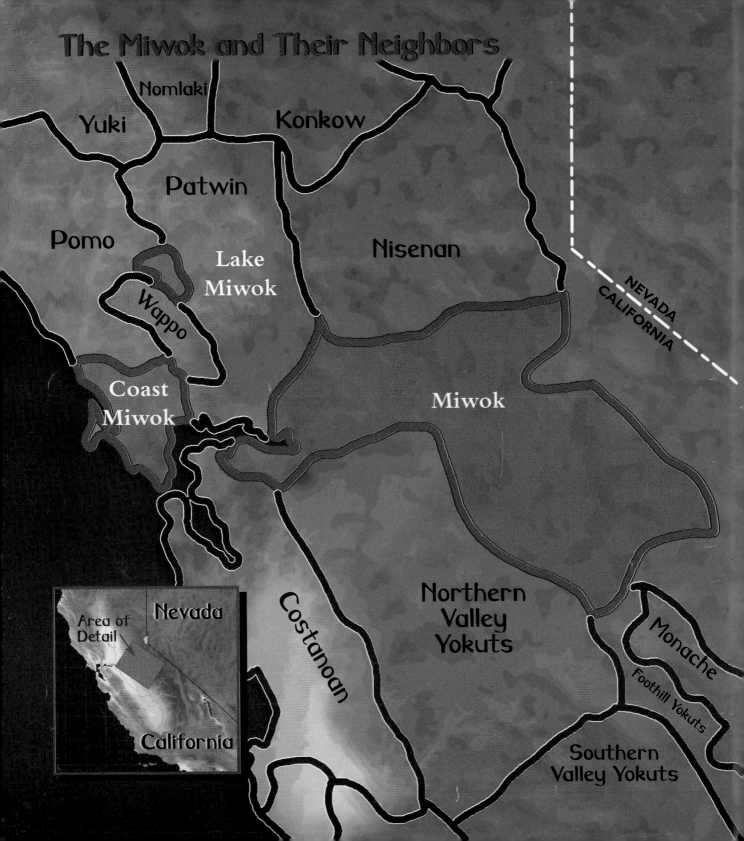

The Miwok and Their Neighbors

Nomlaki

Yuki

Konkow

Patwin

Pomo

Lake
Miwok

Nisenan

Wappo

NEVADA
CALIFORNIA

Coast
Miwok

Miwok

Costanoan

Northern
Valley
Yokuts

Monache

Foothill Yokuts

Southern
Valley
Yokuts

Nevada

Area of
Detail

California

One

Introducing the Miwok People

If someone travels from the Golden Gate Bridge of San Francisco Bay in the west to the towering Sierra Nevada mountains in the east, he or she will see that California is a land with many faces. The coastline is marked by sharp cliffs and towering redwoods. On the shores of San Francisco Bay are enormous reed-choked wetlands. Moving away from the bay to the north, east, and south are grasslands and redwood forests. To the east, the land stretches out toward the horizon, forming a broad grassy plain that ends at the towering Sierra Nevada. Someone who climbs into the foothills will see that the grasslands give way to oak forests. The highest country is filled with dense pine trees and, in some places, giant trees, the sequoias. This amazingly varied land was the ancient territory of the Miwok.

The name "Miwok" was used by the Central Sierra Miwok to identify themselves as a people. Scholars apply the term to the native groups that speak the same basic language, even though they originally used many different names to identify themselves. Most modern Miwok have accepted the term.

The Miwok people can be divided into two large groups that span the state of California in a roughly east-west pattern. In the

This map shows Miwok territory and territories of neighboring tribes.

west are the Coast Miwok and the Lake Miwok. In the east are the Bay Miwok, the Plains Miwok, and the Sierra Miwok. The eastern groups are sometimes called the Valley Miwok. The Sierra group is often broken up into central, northern, and southern groups. When the Europeans first arrived in the area in the sixteenth century, there were more than 20,000 Miwok living in this immense region.

The Miwok developed an amazing way of life that allowed them to adapt to the many environments that they lived in. They suffered horribly as a result of the invasion of their homeland by Europeans and Americans. Despite these fierce challenges, they have survived to become an important part of the modern world.

The origin of the Miwok is surrounded by mystery. The ancestors of the Native Americans arrived in North America before writing was invented. The scholars who study ancient peoples are called archaeologists. Using the evidence that they dig up, archaeologists have created a general picture of the origins of the Miwok.

Most archaeologists believe that the first people to live in the Americas reached the region sometime between 13,000 and 40,000 years ago. These people came from Asia using an ice bridge that connected a series of tiny islands. The people probably came because they were following herds of wild animals, such as caribou. These animals gradually moved over the ice to find grasses and other plants. Eventually, the herds and their hunters found themselves in the northeastern part of North America, while many remained in the

Today, the Bering Strait is a series of small islands between Alaska and Russia. Thousands of years ago, these islands created a land bridge which joined North America and Asia.

The Miwok of California

West. During the hundreds of years that followed, the first Americans moved to the south. They eventually occupied all the available land.

Among these early travelers were the ancestors of the Miwok. Sometime between 3000 and 1000 BC, these native explorers moved into the areas where they would remain. At one time, the

The beautiful Yosemite Valley was part of the Miwok territory. The landscape was rugged and dramatic, yet teeming with vegetation and animal life.

Miwok probably occupied all the land from the Golden Gate to the top of the Sierra Nevada. However, when new native peoples arrived, some of them occupied parts of the Miwok land. By AD 1500, the Miwok territory had been broken into three portions.

Some Native Americans argue that the archaeologists' views are wrong. They insist that the Miwok and other native peoples had always been in the places where they were found by newcomers in the sixteenth century.

Two

Daily Life

The explorers who visited the Miwok territory did not understand the people who they found. Because they were culturally different than European or Asian nations, the explorers argued that the Native Americans were "primitive" people. Today we recognize that the Miwok way of life was both beautiful and practical. The Native Americans' abilities made it possible for them to prosper for thousands of years.

Living in a Series of Different Environments

The Miwok were able to get all the things they needed to survive from the lands that surrounded them. The places where the various groups found themselves had different kinds of resources. The Coast Miwok lived in what today is Marin County and southern Sonoma County. Their livelihood focused on the resources found in the bay, in the ocean, and on the land. The Lake Miwok lived on the shores of the beautiful waters of Clear Lake. They concentrated their efforts on making a living from the water as well as the dry land. The Valley Miwok lived

This painting, done in 1878, depicts what life in the Yosemite Valley might have been like before Europeans arrived in the area.

in a territory of greater variety. The Bay Miwok lived along the eastern portion of San Francisco Bay and in the surrounding hills and mountains. They depended on foods from the bay shores and the nearby landlocked regions. To their east were the Plains Miwok and the Sierra Miwok, whose food resources did not include any that came from saltwater or major lakes.

Nearly all of the Miwok's lands were filled with plants and animals that made excellent food. The larger animals included elk, deer, antelope, and bears. Some of the people also hunted sea otters, seals, and sea lions. The lakes, streams, rivers, and seashores had abundant fish and shellfish. The smaller creatures that were eaten included beavers, rabbits, squirrels, snakes, bats, skunks, mice, wood rats, insects, and birds. Like most other native groups, the Miwok kept dogs, which served as guards, helped with hunting, and were companions. The Miwok also ate many different kinds of plants, including acorns, buckeyes, wild grass seeds, kelp, Indian lettuce, clover, and nettle leaves. The Miwok collected mushrooms, wild grapes, manzanita berries, and other kinds of fruit. They even consumed the seeds of the digger and Coulter pine trees.

Hamlets and Villages

The Miwok lived in settlements with populations that varied from between 20 and 200 people. Most communities had about

100 individuals. There may have been more than 600 Miwok settlements when the first Europeans reached California in the sixteenth century.

There were two basic kinds of Miwok communities. The first group were hamlets. These small settlements contained people who

Most Miwok houses were built with circular or oval designs. The materials for the houses consisted of wood, bark, reeds, mud, and other natural resources.

13

were related to each other through their fathers. The second type of community was larger and was usually called a village. Villages were inhabited by a headman's, or leader's, family, and usually included an assembly hall.

Miwok houses were usually built with a circular or ovular plan. From the outside they looked like cones or domes. Materials from areas adjacent to the village were used to create the houses. In most areas, wooden poles were used as a framework. The walls were built up using reeds, reed mats, slabs of bark, driftwood, grass, branches, or similar clusters of brush. Almost all the homes were dug into the ground and had a central fire pit. This feature was used to cook family meals and to heat the house. The roofs were usually equipped with a smoke hole that allowed sunlight to enter the dark interior. Some houses were covered by earth, clay, and grasses. The doorway was covered with a simple reed mat or hide. The people slept on simple mats that surrounded the fire pit. Some chiefs had special wooden beds and seats made of poles and bearskins.

The headman's village had a larger structure that served as an assembly hall. These buildings are sometimes called roundhouses. A few measured more than 60 feet (18 meters) in diameter. Some roundhouses had clay floors that were 5 feet (1.5 m) deep. Four massive upright logs supported the smaller beams that made up the cone-shaped roof. Each roundhouse had a central opening that served as a smoke hole. A doorway was cut into the side of the structure. In some cases, a person traveled through a long wooden tunnel to enter the structure.

Nearly every Miwok settlement had a sweat house. These buildings were similar to homes. Most measured between 6 and 15 feet (1.8 and 4.6 m) in diameter. They had floors that were 2 to 3 feet (0.6 to 0.9 m) below the surface of the ground. A large fire in the middle of the room filled the sweat house with smoke and intense heat. Men and women used separate sweat houses. The Miwok took sweat baths during healing and religious ceremonies. Hunters also spent time in the sweat house in order to temporarily cover their human smell. This would allow the hunters to sneak up on deer or other animals without being detected. In order to do so, they went into the sweat house and burned strong-smelling plants, such as sage. During their spare time, men and older boys often gathered in the sweat house to talk.

The Miwok built storehouses, or granaries, on the tops of wooden platforms or in the trunks of trees. These small buildings held acorns. The walls were made out of branches and brush. The storehouses protected the food from deer and insects.

The Miwok built temporary shelters using grasses, poles, branches, leaves, reeds, and brush. These structures were used to protect people from the sun, wind, and bad weather. Many of the Miwok moved to temporary camps several times each year to take advantage of changing

food resources. The older people and the smallest children often stayed behind at the main village or in their hamlets.

Cooking

The Miwok women were usually responsible for creating the family meals. They used many different methods to prepare nutritious and tasty dishes. Several types of wild plants and nuts had to be crushed using stone tools, including flat slabs called metates, and rocks with round holes called mortars. In order to grind the food into a powder, the Miwok used smaller stones called manos and cylindrical rocks that are called pestles. Some of the plants, such as acorns and buckeyes, contained natural

The Miwok used storehouses, like the one pictured here, as storage facilities for acorns and other gathered food.

poisons. In order to remove these materials, the Miwok soaked them in fresh water.

Many of the native dishes were prepared like modern stews or porridge. The Miwok did not use pottery or stone bowls. In order to cook a liquid meal, they used watertight baskets. The women stirred in small stones that had been heated in the fire. A large wooden paddle was used to keep the rocks moving. If the hot stones rested on the bottom or at the sides, they often burned a hole in the basket.

The Miwok also used cooking pits to roast their food. The cooks would build a fire in a large hole in the ground. After the flames had been going for several hours, the wood and charcoal would

Miwok women were usually responsible for preparing meals. This Miwok woman gathers plants for cooking.

be removed using sticks. The food was wrapped in small bundles that were placed in the pit. The embers, rocks, and soil were used to cover the hole. After a few hours, the roasted food was unearthed, unpacked, and eaten.

Many of the Miwok foods were prepared using an open fire. The flesh of animals was often cut into thin strips and roasted directly in the glowing coals. Fish, birds, and most other smaller animals were cooked whole in the ashes of the fire.

18　This Miwok cooking site was used to prepare acorn mush.

Meat and fish were often salted and smoked for long-term preservation. The flesh was cut in strips and laid over a wooden rack or branches. A small fire was built beneath the strips. Within a few hours, the meat or fish was ready to be packed away for storage.

The use of bedrock mortars was an important part of the cooking process for the Miwok. This series of holes was made in a limestone bed near the Kaweah River in the Yosemite Valley.

Clothing and Body Decoration

The Miwok people lived in several different types of climates. The people who stayed in the warmer regions wore little clothing. Those who lived in the colder parts of the mountains and foothills covered themselves with a wide variety of outfits.

Nearly all the Miwok males wore small pieces of deerskin, known as breechclouts, suspended from their belts. Hunters sometimes wore animal skins and deer heads. Every Miwok woman wore a skirt, or apron, that covered the lower parts of her body. When the temperature dropped, the people wore blankets or capes made from fur or skin. Some people wore moccasins and leggings.

Both men and women wore different kinds of tattoos. The Miwoks were first tattooed when they were between twelve and fifteen years old. The tattoos were applied using a sharp piece of stone and ashes. During ceremonies, many Miwok wore body paints.

Every Miwok baby's head was tightly bound to a cradle board. This caused the backs of their skulls to develop a pronounced flat appearance. The Miwok believed that this look was very attractive.

The Miwok used many different kinds of jewelry made from shells, bones, and feathers. The nose as well as the ears were often pierced. Young children wore flower earrings. Adults sometimes wore long wooden nose rods.

This portrait, done in 1903, depicts Miwok chief Francisco Gregory in a festive dance costume.

Arts and Crafts

The Miwok had an amazing ability to make things that were both practical and beautiful. Most men and women devoted a part of each day to make the items that they depended on. In some of the larger communities, individuals were given specialized jobs. For example, some men just made arrowheads from a kind of black volcanic glass called obsidian. Other individuals specialized in making things such as shell beads or bows and arrows. These people were paid for their work in other goods, such as shell jewelry and deerskins.

The Miwoks' skill at arts and crafts created a rich and colorful culture. This photo shows a member of the Miwok Nation wearing festive clothing at a celebration in 2003.

Miwok men created hundreds of types of stone tools. The objects the Miwok produced included knives, arrowheads, spearheads, drills, and scrapers. Many of these tools were made by chipping lumps of obsidian, flint, basalt, and other rocks. Some stone tools were created by grinding. The Miwok often used basalt, sandstone, and granite for these objects. Sometimes the heavier grinding stones, like metates and mortars, were left in place when a village was moved to a new location. Some Miwok created deep mortars in rocky outcroppings. These areas are called bedrock mortars.

This photo, taken in the late nineteenth century, shows a Miwok cooking area. The rocky area was used to prepare food.

The Miwok also created smaller stone objects, such as arrow shaft straighteners. These devices had a single groove. The straighteners were made from a special kind of stone, called steatite, that did not crack when heated in the fire. Once they were hot, arrow shafts were passed through the groove in order to remove any curves or other defects.

The Miwok women were amazing basket makers. They produced baskets that were used as trays, fans, jars, dishes, bowls, and even

24 This Miwok woman demonstrates her culture's skill at basket weaving. Today, Miwok baskets are still prized by collectors.

rectangular boxes. The women collected special grasses, rushes, and tree shoots to weave together in many different patterns. By changing materials, the women created dozens of interesting geometric designs. The women further decorated the baskets by including feathers and pieces of shells. Several types of baskets were woven together so tightly that they could hold water and other liquids. Basket collectors from around the world prize the surviving Miwok containers.

The plant world provided other useful raw materials. Wood was transformed into musical instruments, smoking pipes, digging sticks, arrow shafts, bows, spears, bowls, cups, ladles, stirring sticks, trays, paddles, and even house poles. Some plants, such as milkweed and Indian hemp, could be used to make strong threads. These fibers could be woven to create bags, belts, and nets. Reeds were also woven into strong mats and pounded out to make fabric for skirts. Many of the Miwok collected wild tobacco, which they smoked in pipes. The Indians who lived near water were experts at combining willow rods with bundles of reeds to make slender rafts. Every Miwok community had people who knew how to cure certain illnesses using plants.

Animals provided other important resources. Skins and furs were used to create capes, blankets, aprons, belts, skins, bags, breechclouts, and ropes. Bones were transformed into combs, hairpins, needles, awls, beads, gaming sticks, and hammers. Bird feathers were used to create arrows, headdresses, special capes, belts, and jewelry. Even the sinews, or tendons, taken from dead deer were used to make bows.

26 The Miwok were well-known for their skill in basket making. Baskets, like the one pictured here, played many important roles in Miwok life.

Trade

Miwok villages often traded with each other and their neighbors. The items they acquired included salt, shells, deerskins, and special kinds of raw materials that were used to make stone tools, such as obsidian and steatite. The Miwok often paid their trading partners in small shell beads that served as a kind of money.

Three

Other Aspects of Miwok Life

The Miwok used a number of different ideas to organize their society. Membership in a particular group was generally based on whether a person was a man or a woman, how old he or she was, and who his or her father was.

The smallest Miwok social unit was the family. A person was automatically included in his or her father's group when he or she was born. Families were combined into two larger organizations called moieties. These groups were assigned a common animal ancestor, such as a wildcat or coyote. A reference to a person's moiety was usually included in his or her name. No one was allowed to marry anyone from their moiety. The two moieties made up the largest Miwok social unit, which is known as a tribelet.

Every Miwok community had an overall male leader, or headman. They were assisted in their leadership by female religious managers. These females were sometimes called dreamers, or headwomen. The most powerful leaders had assistants that helped them communicate and prepare materials required in community celebrations. Most Miwok villages also had a number of people who served as part-time doctors. These specialists gathered sacred objects that they believed held special powers. The doctors were

As Europeans moved into their territory, the Miwok adopted some of the newcomers' culture. This family, photographed in 1902, wears clothing adopted from outsiders.

respected members of the community. They were also feared because the natives believed the doctors could use their extraordinary abilities to harm people.

Government

The basic unit of Miwok government was the tribelet. A tribelet's territory included food gathering and hunting areas, a main village, and the related hamlets. The population of most tribelets ranged from 100 to 500 people.

The office of headman, or chief, was passed down from a father to his son. Each village headman worked to regulate important aspects of daily life within his community. The headman was also responsible for paying the costs of major celebrations and hosting visitors from outside the group. He was often asked to serve as judge for family disputes. Someone who wanted to use the tribelet's resources had to get permission from the headman. The village headman also provided leadership during wars.

This is a portrait of a Miwok headman taken in 1924. The position of headman, or chief, was passed down from father to son.

Some headmen had a staff of special hunters, fishermen, cooks, and servers. These people generally helped during religious ceremonies or when outsiders were visiting. The headwomen were usually placed in charge of community religious rituals and related activities. The headmen were also served by speakers and messengers. Speakers took orders directly from the headmen and often ruled over the smaller hamlets.

Warfare

The Miwok are a proud people who have always protected their lands against challenges from other native communities and outsiders. Their warriors sometimes launched attacks against other settlements to acquire property and take captives. Sometimes wars broke out when one group accused another of using supernatural powers to cause environmental problems, such as floods. The village headman usually led his warriors in battle. The Miwok used spears and bows and arrows in combat.

During the period between 1769 and 1880, the Europeans introduced horses to the Native Americans. The Miwok were able to tame the horses and learn many new skills. Riding horseback would greatly change the methods used in warfare for the Miwok people. The introduction of guns would also greatly change the landscape of warfare. Unfortunately, both these new methods would open the way for deadlier conflicts between Native Americans and Europeans.

Language

The Miwok share membership in the Utian family of the Penutian language group. Each tribal subdivision had its own version of the Miwok language. Within these divisions, the people spoke many different variations or dialects. These differences were as great as those found between Spanish and English. People from different regions within the Miwok area had a hard time understanding each other.

Religion

The Miwok have ideas about God and the mystical world that focus on the need for preserving the balance between humans and the natural environment. They held religious celebrations on many occasions, including acorn harvests, births, and marriages. The Miwok often prayed for food and other resources. The people gathered in their roundhouses for community worship. During the ceremonies, the Miwok generally sang and danced. Religious leaders wore special body paint, clothing, and colored bird-feather headbands. Human voices provided most of the music. Their songs were sometimes accompanied with the sounds of wooden clapper sticks, hollow foot drums, flutes, and whistles. Many hours were spent teaching the young people community traditions and history. Some religious celebrations also provided opportunities for the Miwok to talk with their friends and play games.

This portrait shows a traditional Miwok fisherman during the early 1900s.

The eastern Miwok marked some rocky outcroppings with intricate designs, such as human tracks, spoked wheels, circles, and similar geometric patterns. These images were lightly carved into the rocks. These types of markings are called petroglyphs. The Miwok did not paint the surface of the rocks—another type of rock art called pictographs. No one knows why the Miwok

34 This photograph, taken on July 4, 1902, shows many Miwok along with newcomers, at a dance.

and other native peoples created these images. Many experts argue that they were made as part of a religious ceremony. Because petroglyphs are sacred to many modern Native Americans, it is essential that everyone show respect when they view them.

The modern Miwok preserve hundreds of different religious stories. Some of the most famous accounts involve a mountain in western California called Mount Diablo. According to many elders, Grandfather Coyote created the native peoples, along with everything that would be needed for life, at this dramatic mountain peak. For this reason, Mount Diablo remains a sacred place to many modern Miwok.

Four

Dealing with the Newcomers

In 1542, some of the Coast Miwok saw the ships of Juan Rodriguez Cabrillo. He was the first European to explore the Pacific shoreline of California. Cabrillo told the native people that he was claiming the region for King Carlos V of Spain, and that it was now a part of New Spain. During the 200-year period that followed, many other Europeans explored the region. Among them was the Englishman, Sir Francis Drake. He stopped in the Miwok region in order to repair his ship before continuing on his voyage around the world. Drake discovered that the Miwok people were friendly and he told them that he hoped to come back some day in order to establish a British colony that he called New Albion. (Albion was an ancient name for England.) His expedition provided the first illustrations and descriptions of the Miwok.

Although the Europeans did not start a colony in California until 1769, the Native Americans who lived in the region were almost certainly affected by the newcomers. The explorers did not realize that they were introducing new diseases, such as smallpox and measles. These

This illustration *(left)* depicts the ship used by Sir Francis Drake during his explorations around the world. This portrait of Drake *(above)* was painted around 1596. Drake would be the first European to greet the Miwok people.

illnesses killed tens of thousands of Native Americans. Although no one described the population losses in California, evidence from nearby territories suggests that as much as 90 percent of the people were killed. The Miwok probably suffered a period of dramatic population loss before they experienced an era of slow recovery.

The Miwok and the Spanish and Russian Empires

In 1769, the first Spanish colony was established at San Diego. California soon became a remote frontier of the Spanish empire. Most

Fort Ross on Bodega Bay was established by the Russians in 1812. By 1841, the Russians had left the fort and sold it to the Americans. Forts like this would allow Europeans to move into the interior of California.

of the foreigners' activities took place in a narrow strip of coastal land that stretched from San Diego to San Francisco. Here they built a chain of military colonies (presidios) and towns (pueblos). They also built missions, which were used to spread Christianity and the European way of life. Although expeditions often journeyed into the interior, the Spanish colonization program was never able to expand into the region. When the Spanish empire in North America ended in 1821, most of the Miwok remained in areas outside of the Europeans' control.

By 1776, a military base and mission were established in what is now San Francisco. A Spanish naval officer, Joseph Cañizares, followed the shoreline into the lands of the Bay Miwok. For the time being, the newcomers and Native Americans got along. The other Miwok groups were protected to some extent by geographic barriers and other Indian nations. However, the missionaries and soldiers were soon exploring their homelands.

In 1812, the Russians established a fort at Bodega Bay. At first, the Coast Miwok enjoyed friendship with them. As time passed, the invaders realized that the Native Americans were not as willing to share their land and work for them. Consequently, they forced many Miwok to work for them as slaves. Fortunately for the Native Americans, most of their efforts were confined to a small section of the coast and nearby valleys.

After 1794, large numbers of Coast Miwok, Bay Miwok, and Plains Miwok were drawn into the missions that stood on the shores of San Francisco Bay. Although the people living in the interior and the north escaped contact with the Spaniards for some time, they were affected by the larger changes that were taking place as a result of the presence of foreigners in California. Many of the old trading networks disappeared. A fresh round of new European diseases killed many Native Americans. Strange new animals, including cattle, horses, mules, sheep, and goats, appeared. They often ate the wild crops and caused other environmental damage. Many Miwok found it difficult to continue their old way of life.

The changing world also provided the Miwok with new opportunities. Many coastal people who lived at the missions ran away and joined Miwok settlements in the interior. These people brought many foreign tools, foods, customs, and new ideas. The Miwok were soon experimenting with growing crops and using the invaders' curious animals.

Spanish horses soon revolutionized the way of life for many Native Americans. The Miwok discovered that they were both a reliable source of food and an excellent method of transportation. Because they increased the distance that a war party could cover, they also revolutionized warfare. For the first time, raiders could bring back large amounts of captured goods and other tame animals, like cattle and mules.

Large-scale warfare with the Spaniards and their mission warriors increased at the end of the Spanish period. In 1812, the Miwok living along the Consumnes River fought a major battle against the invaders. The Spanish troops and mission Indians used boats and

The Spanish would have many bloody conflicts with the Miwok. This sketch, probably done by José Cardero, depicts Native Americans protecting their homeland from a Spanish soldier.

canoes to surprise some 1,000 Plains Miwok. The soldiers' muskets drove the Miwok from the battlefield. Seven years later, another bloody struggle was fought near modern-day Stockton. It ended with the death of twenty-seven Miwok warriors.

The Miwok responded with their own offensives against the missions, soldiers, and settlers. Using captured horses, they struck with lightning speed, running off thousands of head of cattle, sheep, mules, and horses. For the time being, neither side could gain the upper hand in the conflict.

To the north, Chief Marin of the Coast Miwok organized several of the tribelets into a combined force. In 1816, he attacked a column of Spanish soldiers and mission allies with 600 warriors. The Europeans' firepower produced another victory for the invaders. Chief Marin was hauled off to a prison in San Francisco. He soon escaped and made his way back to his homeland. Still, the Spaniards refused to give up. In 1819, Franciscan missionaries finally established an outpost within the territory of the Coast Miwok. The fighting would continue.

The Miwok and the Mexican Republic

By the time the flag of Spain was lowered for the last time in California in 1821, the Miwok way of life had been dramatically changed. Under the flag of Mexico, the native people who had lived on the fringe of the Spanish colony would be confronted by another wave of invasions.

Some of the Miwok were discovering that life at the missions was their only option. For some native peoples, the new mission communities offered an opportunity to find a new, productive way of life. Most of the mission priests worked hard to understand the Native Americans and their needs. They were committed to helping the

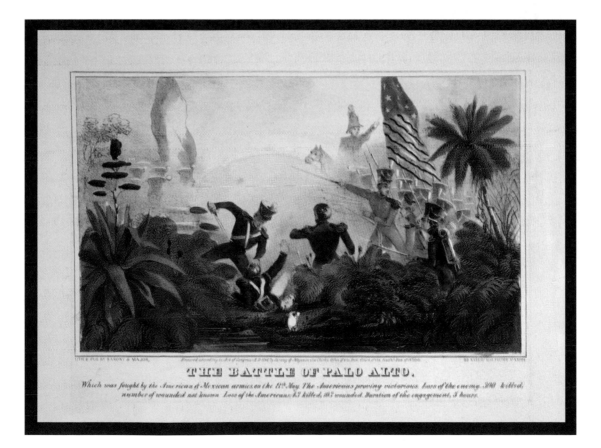

THE BATTLE OF PALO ALTO.

Which was fought by the American & Mexican armies on the 8th May. The Americans proving victorious, loss of the enemy 300 killed, number of wounded not known. Loss of the Americans 17 killed, 107 wounded. Duration of the engagement, 5 hours.

The Battle of Palo Alto marked the beginning of the Mexican-American War. As a result of the war, America would gain large portions of the Southwest, including the Miwok territory.

Miwok however they could. But things often went terribly wrong. It is hard for people who come from different worlds to come together in understanding and friendship. For many Miwok, the future at the missions seemed sad and bleak.

Chief Marin continued to organize resistance among the Coast Miwok. He was joined by Chief Quintin in his efforts. In 1824, the two leaders fought a terrible battle against the Mexicans. This struggle ended in failure and the capture of both Marin and Quintin. Leadership now fell to Chief Pomponio. His efforts ended in a defeat that took place near the modern town of Novato. Pomponio eventually joined the other Coast Miwok leaders in prison at the military base of San Francisco.

The invaders continued to attack Miwok settlements to the east of San Francisco Bay. Expeditions were launched from Mission San José using boats equipped with cannons. In 1826, the Miwok won a battle and killed thirty-six soldiers and mission warriors. The Mexicans quickly mounted another expedition. This time, forty Miwok fell. An even greater number perished in a five-hour struggle fought the next year. Still, the Miwok would not surrender. Several smaller Mexican expeditions were ambushed in 1828. Many Sierra Miwok rebelled the following year. Unfortunately, this revolt, like so many other attempts to preserve native freedom, ended in disaster.

In 1833, all of the Native Americans of central California suffered immense losses due to a malaria epidemic. The disease was spread by mosquitoes. The groups who lived along the shores of the waterways were especially affected.

After 1835, the Mexican government closed down the missions and a new age of savage fighting began. Where missionaries had once sought to influence or win over the Native Americans, the Mexican settlers now wanted the complete destruction of their enemies. The Sierra Miwok continued to resist under chiefs Motti and Zampay. Their numbers grew as they were joined by many former mission residents. After inviting some of the combined forces of Christian and non-Christian Miwok to negotiate a treaty, the Mexicans suddenly turned on their guests and violently assaulted them. The

Miwok who were present were all captured. The 100 Christian prisoners were systematically murdered at the side of the road. The executions were made using bows and arrows, with each victim being shot in the front and back. The few who survived this treatment were finished off with spears. Another 100 non-Christians were baptized and then shot. Still, the worst was yet to come.

One of the most cruel figures to appear during the Mexican era was a Swiss investor named John Augustus Sutter. In 1839, he received a special

All by himself, John Augustus Sutter would bring terrible hardships to the Miwok. Sutter would use many of the Miwok people as slaves to build his own estate.

46 Gold was discovered at Sutter's Mill in 1848 and the California gold rush began. The rush for gold brought huge populations of invaders into the Miwok territory.

license from the Mexican government to set up a private fortress along the Sacramento River. Here he established an immense estate, which was built using stolen native lands and Miwok labor. Sutter used some of the Native Americans as soldiers, others as hired workmen, and an even larger group as slaves. In order to occupy the Miwok's lands, Sutter encouraged other non–Native Americans to build farms in the surrounding valley.

In 1842, the formerly remote Lake Miwok became the focus of the Mexicans' wrath. For the first time, the Native Americans were confronted by soldiers and settlers from the newly founded outposts of Sonoma and Petaluma. Another investor named Mariano Vallejo led an enterprise that rivaled that of Sutter. To Vallejo, the Native Americans were in the way. When the Miwok were accused of stealing a cow from one of Vallejo's properties, a combined force of ranchers and their employees headed for the Clear Lake area. Their assault resulted in the deaths of many Indians and the capture of nearly 300 prisoners. These Miwok were later used as slave labor to harvest the ranchers' wheat.

Mariano Vallejo's greed would rival John Sutter's. Vallejo would enslave hundreds of Miwok, all for the purpose of making a rich man even richer.

During this era, more outsiders appeared among the eastern Miwok. Mountain men were drawn to California in search of furs and trade. These men arrived with a rich variety of goods that they were anxious to exchange for horses, mules, and cattle. The mountain men came from the east and the north. They included Americans, British, and French Canadians. The eastern Miwok were soon collecting wool blankets, glass beads, knives, and other metal objects. They needed to capture more and more Mexican animals to purchase these goods.

The Miwok and the Americans

In 1847, California was conquered by the United States. The discovery of gold in the Sacramento area less than two years later brought a fresh round of invasions to the remaining Miwok homeland. Most of the miners who came to California despised the Native Americans. To them, the Miwok were an obstacle that should be killed or driven away. They gave the Miwok and other California Native Americans the ugly nickname "Digger Indians," as a way of identifying them as an especially backward group. During the next two decades, thousands of Native Americans who lived in the goldfields were rounded up and killed during one of the most shameful episodes of American history. Those who escaped death were often kept as slaves or wandered as beggars.

A small number of the Sierra Miwok warriors attempted to strike back under the leadership of Chief Tenaya. He had been born in the Mono Nation to the east, but he claimed to be the descendant of the original inhabitants of the beautiful Yosemite Valley. His attempt to protect his people led to the Mariposa Indian War of 1851. The United States Army overwhelmed the Miwok and ended the last major armed resistance to the outsiders. Chief Tenaya and his people were forced to move to a reservation near

This is a photo of Mission San José taken in 1866. Military presence at the mission would be used to launch attacks against the Miwok.

Fresno. In 1855, they received permission to return to the Yosemite Valley.

The Native Americans who escaped the full horrors of the miners' invasion found a world that was further modified by the outsiders. The newcomers created terrible pollution that left the land sterile and the water poisoned. Many Native Americans fell to disease.

Some of the Miwok tried to make agreements with the government of the United States. But they were almost always treated unfairly. Any useful lands that were set aside for Native Americans by U.S. officials were seized by other outsiders. Greedy settlers preyed on the nearly powerless Native Americans in order to steal even the smallest items that had any value. Anyone who resisted the whites was likely to be labeled a renegade and

50 This photograph, entitled "Digger Indian Camp," shows the poor conditions the Miwok were forced to live in during the mid–nineteenth century.

shot on sight. The court system protected the invaders from even the most minor punishments.

The people who ended up living on reservations soon learned that they were to be treated as conquered enemies. They were told that their only hope was to learn to live like the whites. The government supported a series of horrible schools in which children were taught to give up their native traditions and were forbidden to speak their own language. By 1870, surviving Miwok wore European-style clothing and used steel tools and many other items that were introduced by the outsiders.

As time passed, many Miwok gave up hope. Only a few of the strongest people were able to maintain native traditions. The law said that they were not human beings, but they knew better. As time passed, more and more whites began to realize how badly the government had treated Native Americans. They joined with Miwok leaders to form friendships and help them. By 1900, the tide had begun to turn.

Five

The Miwok Today

After 1900, things began to improve for the surviving Miwok. Still, the progress was often painfully slow. The United States government finally set aside a few small areas, called rancherías, for the Coast Miwok, the Plains Miwok, the Northern Sierra Miwok, and the Central Sierra Miwok.

Many Miwok and other Native Americans served with distinction in World War I. In 1922, the United States government finally stopped using the racist term "Digger Indians" to describe the Miwok and other California Native Americans. The Miwok celebrated this event by holding a large ceremony where they burnt a dummy made out of straw that they called "the digger." The location where the ceremony occurred in Amador County is still known as the "Place Where They Burnt the Digger."

Partially in recognition of their bravery and sacrifices during the war, the United States granted citizenship to all Native Americans in 1924. Miwok political leaders and their white allies renewed their struggle to reclaim native lands and the Miwok's right to influence their children's education.

Despite all the efforts of the Miwok and their allies, by 1930, the once numerous Miwok nation appeared to have disappeared.

Today, the Miwok are still very active in Southern California. Here, Lanny Pinola *(right)*, a Miwok spiritual leader, performs at a ceremony alongside Sacheen Littlefeather, an Apache.

The Miwok of California

The official government records indicate that only ninety-three Miwok lived on the reservations. But things were about to improve. For the first time, the United States government actually began to pursue laws that were designed to help, rather than hurt, the Miwok. Although there have been many setbacks, the Miwok have grown stronger and more numerous every year since 1930.

54   The Miwok are slowly winning their struggle for identity in this new century. Here, a park ranger talks to Lemuele Green, a Southern Sierra Miwok. In October 2002, many Miwok gathered in the Yosemite Valley to protest the park's renovation project.

Today, the Miwok lands stand transformed by more than 200 years of the invaders' activities. In many places, the villages of the native people have been replaced by skyscrapers and freeways. Even so, a significant number of Miwok have survived. Many Miwok reservations are still in use today in California. Other Miwok groups who are seeking to establish reservations include the Ione band of Miwok Indians and the Federated Coast Miwok people. In all, there are approximately 1,500 Miwok living in these communities. A much larger number of people of Miwok descent live in other places.

The surviving Miwok dress like other U.S. citizens. Their houses and cars are as modern as those owned by the other people living in North America. Although they participate in the modern world, the Miwok remain a proud nation that is anxious for people to hear their true story. Tribal members, such as Steve Walloupe, have worked hard at places like Indian Grinding Rock State Historic Park to help modern Americans learn about his community and its amazing history. The large complex of buildings includes traditional Miwok homes and a ceremonial roundhouse. There are also places where you can try your hand at native arts and crafts, and a fascinating museum. The park even includes Miwok bark shelters where campers can stay. The information Walloupe provides involves both sorrow and accomplishment. It is a vision of a people that inspires respect.

Despite all their adjustments to modern life, Miwok religious practices are still observed. Many less-visible native traditions have also survived. If you visit Indian Grinding Rock State Historic Park in

56 The dig site at Yosemite Park drew many Miwok protestors in 2002. Many believed the dig would ruin sacred Miwok land. Through all their hardships, the Miwok have been able to preserve their rich culture.

September, you can see Miwok people celebrating their ancient acorn harvest ceremonies. You can actually experience traditions that have been observed without a break for thousands of years.

Many Miwok and other native peoples argue that the United States has not lived up to its treaty guarantees. Some of the surviving Miwok communities are working to gain the recognition and respect they deserve. For example, Gregg Harris, an English professor from the University of California at Los Angeles, led his 407-member community of Graton Ranchería to regain its reservation's legal status through the United States government.

The Miwok have been in the forefront of the environmental movement throughout their homelands. Some Native Americans are also working hard to correct inaccurate portrayals of Native Americans that are seen in television, movies, and schoolrooms. The proud Miwok want to be granted the same civil rights given to other Americans. Despite all the problems they have faced, the Miwok want to help build a better future for our nation.

Timeline

13,000– 40,000 years ago	The ancestors of the Miwok nations arrive in North America from Asia.
3000– 1000 BC	The Miwok move into the areas where they are found by Europeans after AD 1542.
AD 1542– 1769	Europeans explore areas where the Miwok live. They introduce diseases that are likely to have significantly reduced the size of the population.
1579	Sir Francis Drake visits the Coast Miwok.
1776	The Spanish establish a military base and mission in San Francisco. During the decades that follow, more and more of the Western Miwok will be drawn into the mission system.
1812	The Russians establish Fort Ross among the Coast Miwok.
1833	A major malaria epidemic causes many deaths among the Miwok.

1835	The mission system ends.
1835–1846	Increasing numbers of mountain men trade with Native Americans living in the interior, including the Miwok people.
1839	John Augustus Sutter builds a large estate and fort on the Sacramento River, producing an era of hardship for the Plains Miwok and Sierra Miwok.
1846–1848	The United States conquers California as a result of the Mexican War.
1849–1850	The gold rush begins in the Sierra Nevada.
1851	The Mariposa Indian War sees the end of armed resistance to the invaders.
1924	All Native Americans are made U.S. citizens.
1958	Many Miwok reservations are terminated by the government. Most will be restored after the government admits it made a mistake.

Glossary

baptism (BAP-tih-zum) A religious ceremony in which someone is inducted into the Christian community.

bedrock mortars (BED-ROK MOR-turs) Large rocky outcroppings with numerous holes that were used to grind nuts and seeds into flour.

hamlet (HAM-let) A small town or settlement.

manos (MAH-nos) Fist-size pieces of stone that are used with metates to grind nuts and seeds into flour.

metates (meh-TAH-tays) Slablike pieces of stone with depressions that are used with manos to grind seeds and nuts into flour.

mortars (MOR-turs) Large stones with holes that were used with pestles to grind nuts and seeds into flour.

pestles (PEH-sulz) Cylindrical stones that are used with mortars to grind nuts and seeds into flour.

renegade (REH-nih-GAYD) An individual who rejects lawful behavior.

sinew (SIN-yoo) A tendon.

sterile (STARE-il) Unable to produce fruit or offspring.

Resources

BOOKS

Campbell, Paul. *Survival Skills of Native California.* Salt Lake City: Gibbs Smith, 1999.

Malinowski, Sharon, ed. *Gale Encyclopedia of Native American Tribes.* Detroit: Gale Group, 1998.

Rawl, James J. *Indians of California: The Changing Image.* Norman, OK: University of Oklahoma Press, 1986.

Stanley, Jerry. *Digger: The Tragic Fate of the California Indians from the Missions to the Gold Rush.* New York: Crown Publishing, 1997.

MUSEUMS

Indian Grinding Rocks State Historic Park
14881 Pine Grove-Volcano Road
Pine Grove, CA 95665
(209) 296-7488

Miwok Archaeological Preserve of Marin
2255 Las Gallinas Avenue
San Rafael, CA 94903
(415) 479-3281
Web site: http://www.mapom.com

WEB SITES

Due to the changing nature of Internet links, the Rosen Publishing Group, Inc., has developed an online list of Web sites related to the subject of this book. This site is updated regularly. Please use this link to access the list:

http://www.rosenlinks.com/lnac/miwo

Index